Sue, Rudy, and the Truth

by David Nguyen
illustrated by Carol Heyer

Practice Decodable 72

McGraw Hill Education

Bothell, WA • Chicago, IL • Columbus, OH • New York, NY

MHEonline.com

Send all inquiries to:
McGraw-Hill Education
8787 Orion Place
Columbus, OH 43240

ISBN: 978-0-02-145057-2
MHID: 0-02-145057-9

Printed in China

8 9 10 11 12 DSS 27 26 25 24 23

When Sue's pals were on trips, they would send her postcards.

Rudy sent a blue postcard. Rudy printed in small letters. Sue could not read his card.

Sue could read "tuna." What more did Rudy print? Sue did not have a clue!

Was Rudy on a ship? Did he catch a tuna fish? Was that true?

Sue used an old magnifying glass. It gave her clues.

Rudy was not fishing. He had eaten tuna sandwiches. That was the truth!